Seeing the Sky

Jane Leonard

Illustrated by Pauline Sumner

Contents

Chapter 1

Learning About Space

The door flew open and Danny burst into the kitchen. "Mom, we're learning all about stars and planets at school. Did you know that the sun is really a star?"

Danny's little brother Ricky followed him in. Mom smiled and poured them each a glass of milk.

"It can't be a star," said Ricky. "It doesn't twinkle in the sky at night."

"That's because the sun is much closer to Earth than the other stars," Danny replied. He reached into his bag and pulled out a book about space. Then he sat down and began to read. Ricky sat at the table beside him and sighed.

"Are you okay, Ricky? How was school?"
Mom asked. Ricky was in first grade.

Ricky shrugged, but didn't say anything.

"He's sad because of his friend Marco,"
Danny said, without looking up.

Mom looked puzzled, so Ricky explained.

"Marco fell off the swing at school yesterday. He had to go to the doctor," said Ricky. "Today he had a cast on his arm. It's bright green. Mrs. Walsh said Marco's arm is special, and everybody wrote their name on his cast. I want to be special, too."

"Oh Ricky, you're special just the way you are!" said Mom. "Why don't you go outside and play? You might feel better."

Danny looked up from his book. "And Mom, did you know stars aren't made of rock? They're hot balls of gas."

Mom laughed. "I think I'm about to learn a whole lot more about space!"

Chapter 2

Amazing Space

A little later, Danny went outside, too. He wanted to look at the sky. Ricky was playing with his basketball. When he saw Danny, he put the ball down and came over.

"What are you doing?" Ricky asked.

"I'm thinking about all the things up there in space. There's so much to learn about our solar system. It's amazing!" Danny replied.

"We have a solar system?" Ricky asked. "What's that?"

Danny smiled. "It's where Earth is in space. *Solar* means *sun*. The solar system is the sun and all the planets that orbit it, like Earth."

"What does *orbit* mean?" asked Ricky.

He liked talking about stars and planets.
It made him feel grown up, like his brother.

Danny walked around him slowly. "It
means to travel around something. I'm
orbiting you right now, just like Earth
orbits the sun. The other planets orbit the
sun, too."

Ricky looked up at the sky, wondering about orbits and planets. "Hey, look!" he said. "It's not even dark, but I can see the moon! Is the moon a planet, too?"

"No, but it is part of our solar system," said Danny. "The moon orbits Earth. Other planets have moons, too. I just read that Jupiter has more than sixty moons!"

Ricky tried to imagine looking up at sixty moons in the sky. "Is Jupiter bigger than Earth?" he asked.

Danny held up one of Dad's golf balls that was lying in the grass. "If Earth was the size of this golf ball, Jupiter would be the size of your basketball."

He held Ricky's basketball next to the golf ball.

Ricky looked at the golf ball. He knew that Earth was huge, so Jupiter must be humongous!

"Could there be people on Jupiter, too?" asked Ricky.

"My teacher says probably not. Jupiter is made of gases, so it doesn't have a hard surface," said Danny. "Earth is made of

rock, which gives us something to live on. Earth has water and air, too."

Ricky looked up at the sky. There sure was a lot to learn about up there. Then he said, "Danny, can I have Jupiter back now? I want to play basketball."

Danny laughed and threw him the ball.

Chapter 3

Pictures in the Sky

At dinner that night, Danny told his parents more about what he was doing at school. "I have to do a project on something I've seen in the night sky. I guess that means the stars or the moon."

"There's more to see than that!" said Dad, serving himself another bowl of soup. "After dinner, let's go out in the yard and take a look."

"Can I come too?" asked Ricky. "Danny is teaching me about Jupiter."

"Sure," Dad laughed.

Outside, Mom spread a blanket on the grass. They all lay down, looking up at the night sky.

"The stars make pictures in the sky," said Mom. "If you connect that group of stars over there with imaginary lines, it looks like a ladle. That's why it's called the Big Dipper."

"What's a dipper?" asked Ricky.

"It's a kind of cup that has a long, straight handle," Mom explained. "It's like

the ladle we used to scoop soup out of the
pot tonight."

"And look, there's Mars. It's one of the
planets," said Dad, pointing.

Ricky looked and looked, but he
couldn't see Mars or any star pictures. He
could only see blurry patches of light.

"Danny," whispered Ricky, "I think Mom and Dad must have eaten too much soup. I can't see a ladle in the sky." Danny tried to show him, but Ricky still couldn't see what he meant. He began to get upset. What were they all talking about?

"Anyway, I've had enough of this star stuff. Who cares about pictures in the sky?" Ricky stood up and went inside.

Chapter 4

Ricky's Eye Exam

While Ricky was brushing his teeth that night, Danny talked to Mom and Dad. He told them that Ricky hadn't been able to see what they'd pointed at.

"Don't worry, Danny," Mom replied. "Ricky's teacher noticed he had some trouble seeing things at school. We've already made an appointment for him to have his eyes checked."

Before bed, Dad told Ricky that he'd have to leave school early on Thursday.

"We're taking you to see an optometrist for an eye exam," said Mom.

"The optometrist will ask you to look at some posters," Dad explained. "He might

use special equipment to see if you need help to see some things."

"Wow!" said Ricky, bouncing onto his bed. "This might be fun."

When Ricky came home on Thursday, he told Danny some exciting news.

"Danny, my eyes are special, just like Marco's arm! I'm near-sighted. That means I need glasses to see things that are far away." Ricky told Danny that the glasses would be ready next week. "I'll even have a special case for them, so I can take them to school!"

"That's great, Ricky," said Danny. "We can look at stars together now."

Ricky smiled. "I thought you, Mom, and Dad were crazy seeing pictures in the sky. Now I'll be able to see them, too!"

Chapter 5

Ricky's New Glasses

A week later, Dad was reading the paper. "Take a look at this!" he said.

Danny leaned over and read aloud.

Comet to Put on a Show

This weekend will be a perfect time to view a comet as it passes through the night sky. Even though the comet is thirty million miles from Earth, viewers in areas away from city lights should be able to see it with the naked eye, starting at 10 p.m. this Saturday night.

"How can an eye be naked?" Ricky giggled.

Dad smiled. "It means that people can see the comet without using binoculars or a telescope. We could drive to that park just out

21

of town on Saturday night. It's away from the city lights, so it should be a good spot to see the comet."

"That sounds great!" Danny said. "I'll go and tell Mom."

"Dad, what's a comet?" asked Ricky.

Dad read some more from the newspaper.

Comets are a mix of dust and icy gases that travel through space. Some people call them dirty snowballs. When a comet gets near the sun, a long tail of dust and gas forms. It streams behind the fuzzy, glowing ball of the comet.

"Will I be able to see all that with my new glasses, Dad?" Ricky was excited.

"I hope so, Ricky," replied Dad. "But sometimes these things look very small.

We may only be able to see a bright fuzzy
ball moving across the sky."

"That would still be much cooler than
seeing a ladle!" said Ricky.

Chapter 6

A Show in the Sky

"All right, boys, we're here!" said Mom
as they arrived at the park.

"Have you got your glasses ready,
Ricky?" Dad smiled.

"Yes," said Ricky. He put his glasses on
and hurried to get out of the car.

Danny looked at his watch. It was
nearly ten o'clock. It was quiet and dark
away from the city.

"Let's go over there," Ricky said,
pointing to a grassy clearing.

"Good idea," said Dad. Soon they were
all sitting on a blanket, gazing at the sky.

"You can see so many more stars out
here than in the city. It's beautiful!"
Danny said.

"Look, Ricky, there's Venus," said Mom, pointing at what looked like a bright star.

"It's a planet," Danny added.

"I can see it!" Ricky cried.

"There's the Big Dipper," said Danny. "See those bright stars in a line over there, Ricky? That's the handle. And those other stars are the cup."

Ricky looked carefully where his brother pointed. This time he could see the bright dots and the shape of the dipper.

"I can see it!" Ricky yelled. "I can see the ladle in the sky! Now I'm just as crazy as all of you." They all laughed.

"We should be able to see the comet any time now," said Dad, checking his watch. They all lay back to watch and wait.

Ricky looked at some bright stars. He was trying to decide what shape they made when he noticed something moving. He jumped up.

"Look!" he shouted. "There!" He pointed at what looked like fuzzy star, only brighter. It was moving across the starry sky.

"Wow, look at the tail!" called Danny. "It's the comet!"

The family gazed at the streak of light
stretching behind the bright, moving ball.
They watched it until it began to fade
from view.

"Your new glasses must be working,
Ricky," Dad said. "You saw the comet first."

"They sure are," said Ricky.

"You saw thirty million miles away!"
Danny laughed.

Ricky smiled. Now he really felt special.

Amazing Space

Many people like to look at stars and planets in the sky at night. Sometimes people can see other things, too.

Constellations

Long ago, people used imaginary lines to connect groups of stars. The stars and lines looked like pictures in the sky. These pictures are called constellations.

People call this group of stars the Big Dipper.

Planets

We can see five planets without a telescope. They are Mercury, Venus, Mars, Jupiter, and Saturn. We need a telescope to see Uranus, Neptune, and Pluto.

Venus looks like a very bright star.

Comets

Comets orbit the sun, just like planets do. Usually we need a telescope to see comets.

We can see some comets, such as Hale Bopp, without a telescope.

Think About the Story

In *Seeing the Sky*, Danny and Ricky both learn about space. Think about these questions.

- What does Danny say the solar system is?
- What does the family see when they look at the sky after dinner?
- Who is the first person to see the comet? What does the comet look like?

To learn more about objects in space, read the books below.

SUGGESTED READING
Windows on Literacy
The Sun
Planets in Our Solar System

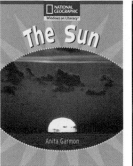

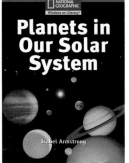